# Applied Psychology

## Volume 10

# TECHNIQUE

# OF

# SUCCESS

Being the Tenth of a Series of Twelve Volumes on the Applications of Psychology to the Problems of Personal and Business Efficiency

## BY

# WARREN HILTON, A.B., L.L.B.

**FOUNDER OF THE SOCIETY OF APPLIED PSYCHOLOGY**

**ISSUED UNDER THE AUSPICES OF
THE LITERARY DIGEST
FOR
NEW YORK AND LONDON
1919**

Republished from the public domain
by

Creative English Publishing

www.Creative-English-Institute.com

Under Classic Reads

May 2014


ISBN-13:
978-1499592900

ISBN-10:
1499592906

# CONTENTS

# OLD MYSTERIES RESOLVED

## Chapter I

## OLD MYSTERIES RESOLVED

### WHAT THE RICH MAN SAYS

IN THE progress of these lessons you have doubtless been troubled with much curious impatience as to the purely practical subject of methods. What you need and what you rightly demand of us are directions as to just how to proceed in your own case.

It is quite in vogue with men who have made their "pile" to point the road for success to others. But the one and obvious fault with their invariable prescription of industry, frugality and temperance is that they furnish no information as how to fill the prescription.

## THE MATTER OF METHODS

In this book we point out the general principles underlying scientific methods, and follow them up with specific rules and directions.

Two difficulties confront us in our endeavor to instruct you in a rational system for increased individual efficiency through mental means. One is the supposed simplicity of mental processes. The other is their supposed complexity.

A great many people, knowing nothing of the psychological discoveries of the past few years, sniff contemptuously at mental procedures. Others are equally insistent that the subject is so profound as to be quite beyond the reach of the average man. Both are wrong.

# AN OLD TOOL PUT TO NEW USES

In the first place, the investigations of recent years have thrown so much light upon old mysteries that every man now has an absolutely definite mental instrument with which to attack the obstacles that hinder his realization of life in its fullness. We are not referring to any new and improved methods for the general training of the mental faculties. The general training of the mind has been widely practiced for generations past. But the time has now come when the mind may be employed with a degree of insight and of scientific accuracy hitherto impossible. The instrument has always been at hand. The advance has been made in the manner and extent of its use.

# SUCCESS AND THE AVERAGE MAN

In the second place, while many problems remain unsolved, there can be no question but that sufficient has been established to make the control of one's mental energies and mental processes an easy matter for any man of ordinary intelligence.

In all that follows, do not for an instant lose sight of the one important truth, namely, that the concentration of consciousness upon a single idea necessarily gives free range to all those impellent energies that tend through bodily activity to transform the idea into a reality.

# THE PSYCHOLOGICAL MOMENT

## Chapter II

## THE PSYCHOLOGICAL MOMENT

### SHUTTER OF THE MENTAL CAMERA

OUR attention is like the shutter of a camera. It may be opened wide to admit the light from all directions, or it may be narrowed to a tiny crevice, so that all that reaches the sensitive plate of your consciousness is a single favored ray. Its range is from zero to one hundred, from perfect indifference to perfect concentration.

There are times when, in a listless lethargy, you float aimlessly with the current of life. At such times your eyes are fixed on vacancy; the hum and bustle of the world melt into a dim confusion; even your own body seems to be far away, and you passively surrender yourself to "the empty passing of time."

Then, again, there are times when you follow a train of thought so intellectually exciting, so fascinating in itself, that you become wrapped in a deep absorption in which you are immune not only to ordinary sensations, but even to pain.

These two states of consciousness may seem to you to be diametric extremes, so far as concentration is concerned. At first thought you would say that the one exemplified the least degree of concentration, and the other the most pronounced. And, in a sense, this is true.

## BOTTLING-UP YOUR FORCES

Yet, in another sense, the two states are closely related. Both are characterized by a very general bottling-up of mental forces. In the first, there is a peculiar and almost complete and indiscriminate restraint of all ideas and impulses. In the second, all ideas and impulses are restrained excepting those embodied in the one absorbing train of thought. In the former, you are "thinking of nothing"; in the latter, you are thinking of one thing with all the mental energy that you possess and to the exclusion of all else.

## COMPELLING ATTENTION

Both these states of mind are as far removed as possible from that voluntary forced attention which is the result of a distinctly felt effort of the will and never lasts more than a few seconds at a time, and also from that other extreme, particularly characteristic of childhood, in which you allow your thoughts to wander here and there at the call of every association that incoming sensory stimuli may arouse.

Comparative concentration is therefore all a matter of emphasis, and ranges with varying degrees of focusing of consciousness from those states of reverie in which nothing is emphasized to those states of purposive thinking in which you concentrate the emphasis of your greatest mental energy upon one subject of thought.

## THE SPOT-LIGHT OF CONSCIOUSNESS

We have elsewhere pointed out that when you concentrate your attention you not only reserve the spot-light of your consciousness for the subject of attention, but you also so arrange your mental forces that all opposing impulses of consciousness are inhibited and your mind and judgment are left free for the consideration of the one subject upon which your attention is concentrated.

It follows, therefore, that the readiness with which your consciousness accepts belief in a given idea depends upon the extent to which contrary impulses are inhibited. In other words, your mental receptivity in respect to one belief is in direct proportion to your mental passivity in respect to all opposing beliefs.

# WHEN MEN WILL BELIEVE ANYTHING

Consequently, and this is of vital importance, a State of general passivity or inactivity of consciousness carries with it an increased credulity, an increased susceptibility to suggested beliefs.

Experiment shows this to be a fact. 'Any arrangement that produces monotony, and so tends to bring about unconsciousness, has a tendency also, and for that very reason, to produce a condition of increased susceptibility to belief. Emotional excitement subsides, memory becomes more random and diffused, consciousness becomes more vague, activity gives way to passivity, and proffered ideas meet with little or no resistance.

## FIRST STEP TOWARD
## IMPLANTING BELIEF

Obviously, if you want to inspire yourself or others with the belief that a certain fact now is or at some future time will be, and to produce at the same time those bodily activities that in themselves tend to work the realization of that belief, then the first step is to bring about just such a passive condition of mind as we have been describing, one in which, as we have just said, "proffered ideas meet with little or no resistance."

For this reason conditions of mental abstraction, such as reverie or such as that half-waking transitional state that precedes sleep, are conditions of great susceptibility to conviction. They are conditions in which consciousness fluctuates from one moment to the next. Now it sinks deep and is merged in sub consciousness; now it rises and mounts to the level of active consciousness. Experiences long past and forgotten drift into view, fresh, living and realistic.

## THE MENTAL CITADEL UNDEFENDED

This means simply that in the absence of any special activity, or, in other words, in the presence of a general inhibition of mental activities, it is readily possible to focus the entire attention upon belief in a given idea. The suggested belief, finding the citadel undefended and meeting with no resistance, takes possession and becomes a permanent part of the mental make-up.

# TENTH LAW OF SUCCESS-ACHIEVEMENT

## Chapter III

### TENTH LAW OF SUCCESS-ACHIEVEMENT

#### JUST WHEN TO FOCUS THE INTEREST

A STATE of reverie and the half-waking transitional stage that precedes sleep are therefore admirable times to practice or induce concentration.

At such moments the mere repetition of an appropriate phrase will so absorb the mind, will so cause the thought embodied in that phrase to be devoured and assimilated, as finally to establish an overwhelming conviction that will subtly influence inner bodily processes and outward conduct.

# HOW TO COMMAND MORE POWER

At such moments, concentrate your mind on the belief in your own ability to achieve things, on your own mastery of conditions, on your own courage to joyfully plunge into the fray, on your own feelings of exhilarating health, and you will presently find yourself assuming a new mental attitude toward the world and your own problems in it. You will find yourself in command of a new and wonderful supply of conscious energy with which to face the issues of life.

Herein lies the secret of the efficacy of prayer and of the powerful emotional appeal of the religious service. The mellow light diffused through stained-glass windows, the deep vibration of the organ's tones, the solemn silence, the bowed head, the atmosphere of peaceful aloofness from the world's alarms — these influences powerfully combine to lull the mind into passivity, into a spiritual receptivity, in which soul-inspiring faiths take root and lift us to a nobler manhood.

# AS TO COINING THIN AIR INTO DOLLARS

Jesus did not attempt to instruct his followers in the mechanical working out of the precepts he gave them. He uttered ultimate truths with the authority of divine inspiration.

He did not attempt to explain just how the prayer of the faithful would work its own fulfilment. He told them the simple truth in words that shepherds and fishermen could understand,

"Faith," he told them, was the mental attitude essential to success. " Therefore I say unto you," said the Master, "all things whatsoever ye pray and ask for, believe that ye have received them, and ye shall have them."

These words are pregnant with scientific truth. They do not mean that gold dollars and automobiles will be materialized out of thin air before your very eyes. They mean that through faith in the realization of your goal you will be inspired with those qualities which tend to compass its attainment.

For inspiration is not the monopoly of any privileged class. The clerk or salesman may be as fervently inspired as may the poet.

# THE MANNA OF THE FAITHFUL

Inspiration, whether of artisan or artist, is concentration. It is the concentration of all one's energies and abilities upon a single point, a single point that for the time represents all the world beside.

With concentration, your mental energies, instead of being scattered over all the world, find themselves centered in a single object. With concentration, that object is magnified. It is illumined. It is brought out in bold relief. It takes form. It moves. It is a living thing.

This is inspiration. This is the manna that drops from heaven into the soul of him that prays in faith. This is mental concentration upon a beloved ideal.

# ELEVENTH LAW OF SUCCESS-ACHIEVEMENT

## Chapter IV

### ELEVENTH LAW OF SUCCESS-ACHIEVEMENT

#### HOW TO DOMINATE OTHERS

GIVEN a state of mental concentration, which of course involves "belief," and the belief upon which the powers of the mind are trained may relate to any subject, may be harmful or beneficial, may come from without or be prompted from within.

A whispered phrase addressed to one in a state of concentration of attention will induce him to act as you desire.

Child-training is almost wholly a matter of concentration of attention.

# HOW TO MOLD CHARACTER

By precept and example we instil beliefs and impulses. The extent to which they take root depends upon the extent to which we have succeeded in so concentrating the attention of the child as to leave no room for the development of contrary and diverting tendencies. Thus are the seeds of character sown.

Most children are never taught to concentrate. Not until compelled by the pinch of necessity do they exercise the will in control of the attention. As children, under the guidance of others, they have no deep interest in anything; they scatter their energies; they never concentrate their minds.

Indeed, many parents are possessed of the foolish notion that sustained intellectual activity along one line would be harmful to the child — as if the concentration of all the mental energies upon one subject at a time involved any more or as much outlay of energy as the ceaseless flitting from one thing to another, the holding of numerous dimly lighted interests before the mind at the same time!

In consequence, the average child grows up "scatter-brained," without any training or ability in such thought concentration as involves the full utilization of subconscious memories and energies.

## THE MAKING OF A PRODIGY

What can be done by a rational system of mind-training in children is evidenced by all the child "prodigies" in history. That James Watt was solving problems in geometry at the age of seven; that Alexander Pope was a master of literary style at sixteen; that Colburn at the age of six could multiply four figures by four figures in nine seconds; that "Blind Tom" and "Marvelous Griffith" were respectively marvels of precocity in music and mathematics, does not prove that these men's minds were inherently better adapted to music, literature and mathematics than the mind of the ordinary person. Such men as Benjamin Franklin, Safford, Ampere, Gauss and the Bidders, all infant prodigies who in later years became famous in many different fields, are evidence to the contrary.

Dr. Sidis, the noted psychologist, whose son recently entered Harvard at fourteen and astonished his teachers by his profound grasp of a variety of Sources of subjects, insists that his son is just an average boy whose interest and attention have been systematically trained.

## SOURCES OF DISTRUST

As the years increase the susceptibility of the individual to the control of his attention by influences from without becomes less and less.

Experience in the competition and strife of life changes the mental disposition.

Men instinctively guard themselves against the lures of others by building up a protecting wall of mental inhibitions.

They become cautious, suspicious. All their past experience is an inhibitory influence causing them to instinctively distrust and repel ideas that are presented by others for acceptance and belief.

# HOW TO CONVINCE THE INCREDULOUS

And yet the most incredulous and cynical of men still retains some degree of credulity. And the success of your effort to implant a desired belief in his mind depends upon the artifice with which your purpose is concealed, the skill with which your hook is baited.

A friend shows you two squares of equal size, one containing a large number, the other a small number. He asks you which is the larger square. If you are a person whose attention is easily controlled by others, your mind will seize upon the comparative sizes of the two numbers, and you will believe that the square containing the larger number is in reality the larger square.

# THE ART OF CROSS-EXAMINATION

Concentration of the other person's attention upon some irrelevant matter is the first aim of every sleight-of-hand performer. It is equally a prerequisite to the success of any man, however high his calling, who seeks to mold the opinions of those forearmed with distrust against him.

Every trial lawyer knows how much depends in cross-examination upon his ability to catch the witness off his guard. He will ask the witness if the number of persons present at the time referred to was four or five. If he has held the attention of the witness to the suggested numbers, the witness will decide for one or the other, although the number of persons present may actually have been six.

# THE TWO WAYS TO WIN MEN

Obviously, the success of your effort to sway the belief and so to influence the will of another depends upon the momentary degree of equilibrium of his consciousness.

If his attention is a free and discriminating agent, the whole weight of his past experience may be massed either with or against the acceptance of the belief you suggest. And this weight of experience is an unknown quantity to you. You cannot foresee upon which side of the scale its influence will be felt.

If, on the other hand, you first soothe his consciousness into passivity, and then concentrate it upon the proffered thought, all his mental energies will be bent upon accepting and assimilating the desired belief.

There are two principal ways in which this concentrative process may be successfully employed:

{a) The first is by working to overcome inhibitions, to remove distrust, to allay fears.

{b) The second is by working to emphasize the goal to be won, dwelling upon its advantages, portraying it in ideal colors.

Each method has its advantages, and both should be used concurrently.

---

You have commonly assumed that as a conscious being you are a free agent, and that being ambitious of success in a given direction you can set out upon the path guided by such financial, economic and ethical principles as you may choose to adopt.

## FIRST STEP TOWARD THE FINAL GOAL

Alas, what a mess you make of it! Instead of pushing straight ahead toward your destination, you soon find yourself straying in a forest of distracting ideas, emotions, desires and impulses. The will-o'-the-wisp of temptation and desire calls to you on every hand.

Some there are who succeed in holding to a general direction. Most of us grope forever without star or compass among enticing interests that lure us from our purpose.

First of all, then, you must remove conflicting desires and emotions that have the effect upon your main purpose of repressions and inhibitions.

## SCIENCE OF RETROSPECTION

This would seem to involve introspection on a large scale. And much is said about the evils of introspection as productive of self-consciousness.

But there are two kinds of introspection. One is purposeless, idle, emotional and depressing. The other is purposive, a thoughtful study of one's self, made with a view to learning the facts, so that those tendencies needing correction may be corrected.

Through such self-investigation, you may scrutinize the obstacles in your own disposition and habits. You may learn to estimate them, without emotion and without self-reproach, at their true value as the manifestations of misdirected energy.

You may find undue fondness for certain pleasures. You may find wasteful habits of emotional excess. You may find moods and fears and undesirable feelings toward those about you.

## THE MAN WHO BROODS

You are very apt to find a morbid self-consciousness, a habit of comparing yourself with others, as if the great achievements of others somehow spelled the story of your own failure and incompetence.

All men experience reverses of fortune. Here and there is one who broods over his failures.

He keeps thinking about himself and his misfortunes until presently he has acquired an "ingrowing disposition."

Instead of releasing his concentrated energies upon an affirmative purpose, he holds them in leash under the spell of an inhibitory and negative idea.

## "INGROWING" DISPOSITIONS

Instead of courageously attacking this negative idea, he says, "Walk right in, Mr. Gloom, and let me have a look at you."

He recounts again and again the circumstances and sensations that attended at the birth of this idea. And the idea draws to itself a multitude of associations and grows into the huge proportions of a mighty mental complex.

Thoughts of discouragement, and thoughts deprecatory of your own self-mastery, never will pursue you unless you entertain them.

But every time you permit them to remain in your consciousness they take on new associations from the surrounding ideas and sensory images in which they find themselves.

# THE COMPLEX OF INEFFICIENCY

And every new association added to the complex of inefficiency makes it so much the more readily recalled to consciousness at another time.

So it comes about that it is the man who lacks the spur of actual want, the man of comparative leisure, who is most apt to fondle ideas of hesitation and incompetency, of doubt and fear.

If introspection reveals these things to you, you will now realize that they are merely mental habits, merely misdirected mental energies, and, looked at in a proper light, evidences of unguessed power that, put to work, will lead you on to fortune.

And, having dragged the skeleton from its closet, you will perceive that failures and defects have no prescriptive right to bar your way to a larger measure of achievement.

## THE DEAD HAND OF DISPARAGEMENT

You will loosen the clutch of the dead hand of self-depreciation. You will fix your thoughts upon a definite goal.

You will refuse to entertain ideas hostile to your purpose. You will quit thinking about yourself. You will banish all fear-thoughts. You will awake to the knowledge that you are supreme in your own mental kingdom.

And so, having taken the first step, having freed yourself from the impediment of useless baggage, you will take the second step, you will plunge into the fight.

## SECOND STEP TOWARD
## THE FINAL GOAL

For merely to inhibit certain unprofitable desires and emotions from conscious activity is not enough. Taken alone it is impossible. There is within you a world of mental energy demanding outlet.

You must, therefore, have recourse to our second concentrative method — that is to say, you must substitute a new group of mental images or pictures in place of those on which unprofitable emotions thrive. You must substitute thoughts in harmony with your purpose.

Consciousness, as you have seen, is but a composite of memory images and their associates. You must see that these images are in harmony with your ideal.

# TWELFTH LAW OF SUCCESS-ACHIEVEMENT

## Chapter V

## TWELFTH LAW OF SUC-CESS-ACHIEVEMENT

### ART OF AFFIRMATION

HERE are two ways by which you may arrange a content of consciousness in conformity with your ideals, (a) One way is by Affirmation in a half-waking state; (b) The other, by Visualization in a half-waking state.

The primary purpose of both methods is the concentration of consciousness. What you want to do is to hold constantly before your eyes the picture of the thing you want to have or to do, the sort of man you want to be.

## THE POWER OF A PLEDGE

Affirmation is of wonderful efficacy in this respect. To declare that the ideal is already an accomplished fact, is already true, is already the greater power within you, is already determining your conduct and controlling your destiny, is necessarily to hold these thoughts in your consciousness and so to inhibit all contrary and conflicting impulses.

When we say that a person speaks "without thinking," we mean that he speaks without previous reflection. There can be no speech without a concurrent activity of the spoken thought in consciousness.

# PSYCOLOGY OF WORDS

Words are a mighty instrument.

They have perhaps more influence upon the speaker than upon the person spoken to. They focus the energy of consciousness.

Strong words strengthen. Weak words weaken. Why? Not because of any magic potency in words as words. But because a word, by its very definition, is "the sign of an idea."

Words express thoughts. Consequently, to affirm the qualities that you desire, presupposes at least the momentary life in consciousness of the mental attitude you have been trying to create.

So if you say to yourself, "I will do this thing," your energy will follow your words.

Affirmation, therefore, presages action. It proves to you the efficiency of your own will. It gives you confidence in your own self-mastery.

## FORCEFUL TALKING
## AND EFFECTIVE DOING

If you find it difficult to control your thoughts, if they persist in fluttering about over an area as wide as the eternal cosmos when they ought to be concentrated upon a single object, try controlling your words.

Talk of your business, talk of your work, talk of your aims, talk of your ideals.

You will find that your thoughts will cluster around your words like grapes about a stem.

You will find that while you are talking of your ambitions, while you are affirming your ideals, while you are pledging the fulfilment of your promises, the eternal laws of Nature are quietly, silently working to bring about the fruition of your hopes.

## IS THIS A PANACEA?

Yet affirmation, fruitful as it is, is essentially a complementary method. It should not be used alone. It may even be overdone. It may be carried to such extreme as to result in a comfortable disregard of the actual facts of existence.

This may be contentment, but it is not life. You were created for nobler things than a bovine serenity. You must not rate this practice of affirmation as anything more than it pretends to be, a mental device, a practical aid to mental concentration.

# A WORKABLE MENTAL DEVICE

There are those among present-day cults and oc-
cults who lift affirmation into a distinct
metaphysical doctrine. Observing the good
results in the form of an awakened will and self-
reliant courage that flow from the practice of
affirmation, they have jumped at the conclusion
that poverty, disease, old age, death and all
things undesirable are in fact as well as in
affirmation non-existent. There have been some
hundreds, perhaps even thousands, who have
passed into the Great Beyond vigorously denying
sickness, pain and death to the last conscious
breath.

Wherein lies the error? Simply in this: that these
people cannot " see the wood for the trees." Like
the naturalist who examines a butterfly, they
have held the practice of affirmation so close to
the eye as to lose all sense of proportion, all
appreciation of true beauty and significance.
They have mistaken the froth for the substance.
They have strayed from the path of scientific
analysis and are lost in a metaphysical forest of
sounding terms, such as "ego," "error," "mortal
mind," "love vibrations," "spirit," and "cosmos."

We do not mean to scoff at any form of religious
belief. Every man is entitled to the undisturbed
enjoyment of the benefits of his special faith. All
are useful. Each is adapted to a special grade of
intelligence.

But to you who are versed in the elements of psychology and familiar with mental processes we say, "The practice of affirmation need not he made the basis of a religious doctrine. It will be just as effective if you know it and use it for just that thing that it is — a mental device, workable and startlingly efficacious, but still essentially a device."

# THE ART OF VIZUALIZATION

A still greater method is Visualization, the practice of creating in imagination the condition to which you aspire.

We are all inclined to give our imaginations free rein in dwelling on our "troubles" and the difficulties and obstacles that we see ahead.

Nothing is easier than to exaggerate difficulties. This looking on the dark side of things, this seeing only the obstacles that strew the way, is what makes the road to success and health so steep for many of us.

But no marksman ever made a bull's-eye while looking at his rival's score. If you want success and health, you must keep your imagination working for you, not against you.

Picture to yourself the thing you want to have or to do, the man you want to be.

# THE MENTAL VISION

When you are about to face a particularly difficult situation, sit down alone in your office, close your eyes, make yourself oblivious to all sensations. Drive all other thoughts, all distractions, from your mind. Create a mental picture of yourself in just the situation you expect to occupy. Embellish it with all possible details. Make the picture as realistic as you can.

Then, see yourself facing the situation meeting the experience, in just the way that you should like to meet it. See yourself confident, adroit, tactful, bold, persuasive. See yourself being the man you want to be, getting the thing you want to have. See yourself happy, successful, triumphant.

And when you awaken from this voluntary looking into your own self-consciousness, you will find yourself in possession of just the qualities you need.

When you come to meet the realities of your mental picture, you will find these outside realities so bound up by association with your own previous mental images that all your impulses will be the impulses associated with your mental picture, and you will naturally and automatically play the part that you assumed.

Self-confidence, address, assurance, boldness, persistence, all are but mental attitudes. Hold them in consciousness as part of a mental picture of yourself in a given situation, and if ever that situation is realized in the physical world, the associative processes of your mind will automatically re-create in consciousness just the mental attitude that characterized you in that picture built of the "stuff that dreams are made of."

This method may be applied to any trait or quality, to any phase of character, to any issue in life, to any condition of mind or body in which changes are desirable.

By Visualization you create associations that will help you to realize the conditions you picture. By your thought you create a mental atmosphere that will find expression in achievement. And this mental atmosphere is nothing more nor less than the makings of character.

Set aside as times for Affirmation and Visualization, as your periods of exaltation and inspiration, the drowsy moments that precede sleep and the half-conscious moments in the morning when you are not yet fully awake.

In the stillness of early morning or in the brooding hush of the night, away from the stress and excitement of the day, with the body in reposeful relaxation, you can mass the powers of your mind in a most vivid visualization of the things you hope to have, to be and to do. Mental images will stand forth in bold relief. You will know then that you receive the inspiration you pray for.

Doubtless at such moments you are in more intimate communion with the Universal Spirit. Doubtless your mind discerns more plainly the way to God's limitless abundance of faith. Certainly resources beyond the reach of your waking consciousness are made available.

We are not here advocating simple meditation. Meditation and reflection unquestionably have their beneficial effects. But Visualization is a vastly different thing.

Visualization deals wholly with the future. Visualization deals with concrete and practical life problems. Visualization deals with action. Visualization makes you a leading character in a drama of your own making. Visualization sets the stage and gives the characters their exits and their entrances. All you furnish is the "happy ending."

To use a different figure, Visualization draws the plans and writes the specifications for your "castle in Spain"; Association is the builder that takes these plans and works them out into a splendid structure of reality.

This practice of visualization will do more than mold your character. History abounds in instances of specific successes achieved unwittingly in the same way. Coleridge awoke with the rhythmical lines of "Kublai Khan" upon his lips. Joan of Arc led the victorious armies of France in accordance with the vision in her father's garden. L Robert Louis Stevenson habitually sought in reverie the material for his romances. Wagner in states of reverie heard the motives of his masterpieces.

A distinguished inventor of today; has brought this practice of visualization to a system, sitting for that purpose in the same chair at certain hours while working out inventions.

First, fill your mind with material. Gather all that observation and reason can give you on the problems in hand. Then, lay aside all worry and fret and anxiety, remove yourself from distracting influences, relax, become passive, give yourself wholly to concentration.

And after a little practice your trained and sensitive consciousness will unravel step by step the tangled skein of any difficulty and weave a pattern that you may reproduce successfully in objective reality.

# THE TWELVE RUNGS IN THE LADDER OF ATTAINMENT

## Chapter VI

### THE TWELVE RUNGS IN THE LADDER OF ATTAINMENT

#### TWELVE RUNGS IN THE LADDER OF ATTAINMENT

BEFORE taking up the exercises that tell you what to do, read again these twelve fundamental laws for Success-Achievement. They are a twelve-runged ladder of attainment.

I. All human achievement comes about through some form of bodily activity.

II. All bodily activity is caused, controlled and directed by the mind.

III. The mind is therefore the instrument that we must employ in the accomplishment of any purpose.

IV. You have hut one mind, hut it is a mind with phases of consciousness and phases of sub consciousness.

V. Your consciousness is made up in part of present sensory experiences and in part of complexes drawn from sub consciousness.

VI. Your sub consciousness is a reservoir of classified complexes, made up of ideas, emotions and motor impulses.

VII. The presence of any idea in your consciousness tends simultaneously to produce an associated "feeling" and to impel you to certain appropriate muscular activities.

VIII. The attention determines what ideas, emotions and motor impulses shall be active in consciousness.

IX. Concentrate the attention, and you automatically control all bodily activities.

X. A state of reverie and the half waking transitional stage that precedes sleep are therefore admirable times to practice or induce concentration.

XI. A whispered phrase addressed to one in a state of concentration of attention will induce him to act as you desire.

XII. There are two ways by which you may arrange a content of consciousness in conformity with your ideals: (a) one way is by Affirmation in a half-waking state; (b) The other, by Visualization in a half -waking state.

# THE FIVE EXERCISES FOR CONCENTRATED PSYCHIC POWER AND INITIATIVE

## FIRST REGIME

### Chapter VII

## THE FIVE EXERCISES FOR CONCENTRATED PSYCHIC POWER AND INITIATIVE

## FIRST REGIME

### DESPONDENCY, TIMIDITY, INDIFFERENCE, INERTIA

THE exercises here set forth, if faithfully pursued, will strike off the shackles of doubt, despondency, timidity, inattention, indifference, laziness, inertia, distracting influences and wasteful emotions and desires, will release you from the fetters of failure and will give you that full measure of success justified by your native ability.

## WHERE THE TROUBLE LIES

If any of these exercises seem too simple, too easy and specific, if you are tempted to regard them as inadequate, we can only say, "You know these procedures are scientifically sound. Try them; the results will amaze and gratify you. Remember the miracles of hypnotic suggestion; the fundamental principle is the same."

Most problems are easily solved if you know just where the trouble lies. One day a friend of mind invited a number of guests to go for a sail with him in his motor-boat on the Sound. When we had reached a point about five miles from shore suddenly the engine gave a few fluttering gasps and "died." After fruitless efforts with a "compressed-air" starter, my friend tried "cranking" the engine in the old-fashioned way. When his arm gave out other men in the party "turned over" the engine until all were exhausted. At the same time spark-plugs were inspected and valves opened and shut until there seemed nothing left to be done but to take the engine apart and put it together again. Meanwhile the ladies shivered and the hours flew by. Finally a passing boat hailed us and the engineer came aboard to help if he could. The first thing he did was to open the gasoline tank. He found it empty. He replenished the tank from a five-gallon can carried in our boat for just such emergencies, and away we went. So it is that the most difficult problem is often the simplest.

# A MAN AND A CORD OF WOOD

In every problem there is a place where the trouble lies. No progress can be made until that spot is found. Effort spent in other ways is wasted. The cause of the difficulty must be found and removed.

Your innate power of accomplishment depends upon the quality and quantity of your psychic energy.

But power of accomplishment is not accomplishment. Capability is not achievement.

Achievement means doing. It means not only the possession of energy, but the liberation of energy.

A cord of wood contains a certain number of heat units. But the spark of combustion is needed to set them free.

In all the world of matter inertia reigns supreme. It is mind action, and that alone, that can perform the miracle of overcoming this inertia and releasing stored-up energies.

# THE INITIATIVE OF THE CLERK

And the mind action that does this must be, and in the very nature of things is, Initiative.

Without initiative the giant is helpless. Without initiative the Napoleon of Business is a man of wood.

Initiative pulls the trigger of muscular discharge.

Initiative is the inevitable source of every manifestation of force.

There are kinds and degrees of initiative.

First, there is the initiative that comes from without. The clerk moves at his master's command.

## THE INITIATIVE OF THE PROMOTER

Second, there is initiative from within — the initiative of ideas, the initiative that arises from an inborn mental impulse, the initiative that is inventive, creative.

Initiative of the first class is the result of motor impulses in the nature of responses to outward sensory stimuli. It is a low order of initiative. It is the initiative of the trout leaping in muscular response to the shimmering of the fly. It is the initiative of the pack-horse obeying the driver's order.

Initiative of the second class comes from within. It is the impellent force of an idea that is vivid, realistic and absorbing. It is the action-producing power of thought complexes forcing their way into every corner of consciousness. This is the initiative of the inventor, the poet, the promoter, the syndicate-head, of all men whose dreams find adequate expression, of all men who build "air-castles" as the first step in the building of castles of steel and stone.

# CLASSIFYING YOUR OWN INITIATIVE

What kind of initiative do you possess?

1. Do you neither see the thing to be done when it is pointed out to you nor act even when told to act? Then, you are no better than a cord of wood.

2. Do you see the thing to be done only when it is pointed out to you and act only when someone tells you what to do? Then, you are but one of untold millions and only a step higher than the faithful pack-horse.

3. Do you see what you ought to do without being told, but either fail to try it or lack the driving force to push it to accomplishment? If so, you are an impractical dreamer. The fact is even your dreams are not clear, definite and dynamic. You do not see what ought to be done here and now, first and most of all. You waste your thoughts on indefinite longings and "glittering generalities."

4. Do you without being told see clearly just what you must do now to succeed, and then do it yourself? Then, you are an enterprising man, a "hustler" and a success, but you are sadly limited in your scope of operations and you will never get very high in the world, since you fail to utilize the most potent means of accomplishment, the activities of others.

# BENDING OTHERS TO YOUR WILL

5. Do you without being told see clearly just what must be done now for the accomplishment of your purpose, and do you cause it to be done by bending others to your will? Then, you are indeed a master of men and of things, and your measure of achievement will be limited only by the breadth and power of your creative vision.

## THE MAN IN A RUT

Someone has said, "The principal obstacle in the way of original thinking is the habit of living in fixed channels, and must be removed at once, because we shall never become any more than we are, so long as we live, think and act according to prescribed rules and preconceived ideas. No growth, no development and no advancement can possibly take place while we live and move in grooves."

Therefore, if your initiative is of the first type, or of any type except the highest, you must make it your business to advance to the next higher type, and so on, step by step, until you shall have reached the seats of the mighty.

# UNSEEN FORCE THAT MOVES THE WORLD

If you are on the first level of initiative, you must climb up to the second and be looking ahead to the third, for "to be a follower is to prevent further growth. No mere follower can ever become great, because he is every day becoming smaller."

All things are possible to him who ardently desires.

Therefore, set your soul upon acquiring the highest degree of initiative. Such initiative is inspirational. It breathes into others the living fire of action. It is the unseen force that moves the world.

# THE FIVE EXERCISES FOR CONCENTRATED PSYCHIC POWER AND INITIATIVE

## SECOND REGIME

### Chapter VIII

### THE FIVE EXERCISES FOR CONCENTRATED PSYCHIC POWER AND INITIATIVE

### SECOND REGIME

### TAKING AIM

YOU cannot accomplish anything until you first determine definitely just what it is to be.

---

A mere general wish for success in one line or another will never do. Every man has, in more or less hazy fashion, that general desire.

Before you summon all the forces of your being to a concerted attack be sure that you know just what you want, what one thing most and first of all.

# FORMULATING A CONCRETE DESIRE

You are called upon to specify, to specify definitely and immediately, the one big thing.

What one material thing do you most ardently desire? What one personal trait or quality do you at once require for the attainment of your highest ambition?

No one can solve this question for you. You must yourself create this factor. You must yourself clearly and definitely resolve and formulate before you can create.

# THE FIVE EXERCISES FOR CONCENTRATED PSYCHIC POWER AND INITIATIVE

## THIRD REGIME

### Chapter IX

## THE FIVE EXERCISES FOR CONCENTRATED PSYCHIC POWER AND INITIATIVE

### THIRD REGIME

#### HUSKS AND GOLD DOLLARS

IF YOU formulate your desire upon a basis of misinformation and half-baked facts, the result will be misapplication of energy and half-baked success. You cannot feed the mind on husks and expect it to turn out gold dollars. It is not an alchemist's crucible to take the poverty of slothfulness and transform it into the wealth that is industry's reward.

## A FACTORY AND ITS RAW MATERIALS

With effort you can have the best that the world has to offer.

Your mind is a mighty structure filled with all kinds of intricate machinery. It is built to turn out the most wonderful of products, success and riches, health and happiness. And you are its master. You can direct its operations and determine the character and quality of its output. But you must furnish it with raw materials appropriate and ample.

And these raw materials are facts.
1. Attention.
Perception is the first step in mind-building.

The senses dig up all the raw material of the mind-life.

Yet how few people there are who attend fully and intelligently to their sensory messages.

## THE ART OF WATCHING

There is all the difference in the world among men and women in this respect. Some have a superficial knowledge of many things; others have but a smattering of one. A few there are who perceive not only outward aspects, but inner content and deep significance.

Says Professor Scripture, "Eyes and No-eyes journeyed together. No-eyes saw only what thrust itself upon him; 'Eyes was on the watch for everything. Eyes used the fundamental method of all knowledge — observation."

"This is the first lesson to be learned — the art of watching. Most of us went to school before this art was cultivated, and alas! most of the children still go to schools of the Same kind. There are proper ways of learning to watch, but the usual object-lessons in school result in just the opposite. We, however, cannot go a step further till we have learned to watch."

# USING THE EXPERIENCE OF OTHERS

2. Make systematic use of your sense organs.
(See Studies in Volume Four.)

3. Fix ideas by their associates.
(See Studies in Volume Four.)

4. Search systematically and persistently.
(See Studies in Volume Four.)

5. The instant you recollect a thing to be done, do it.
(See Studies in Volume Four.)

6. Learn to ask questions.

# THE ART OF ASKING QUESTIONS

One of the most valuable things a man ever learns, and what saves years of effort, is the utilizing of the knowledge and experience of others. It may take a man ten years to learn a thing, but it requires only a minute to tell it. If you ask a question that will draw out his convictions, you can get the same conclusion you would probably reach if you went over the same ground that he did. You can begin where he left off.

The inventor spent thirty years in perfecting the telephone, but you can pick it up and use it in an instant. If you had to invent one yourself before you could use it, you would lose valuable time doing something that has already been done.

Of course, it is to be understood that you should not ask stupid or impertinent questions, as that would cost you the confidence of the person you ask and shut off the help he might be willing to render you.

# HOW TO INVESTIGATE
# A NEW PROPOSITION

Questions that bring out the best information are specific questions thoughtfully asked, and sometimes involving fundamentals. Practice trying the different kinds of questions until you learn which are the best. Asking intelligent questions is an art — in fact, it is an accomplishment.

7. Get the habit of Thoroughness.

Make it your business to examine each new proposition from every side. Study every proposed transaction until you understand it inside, outside, bottom and top and all the way round. Get at the real facts stripped of all uncertainty. Never guess, assume or take for granted. Know— and know thoroughly.

# THE HAIR-TRIGGER SPIRIT IN BUSINESS

If you have but a smattering of knowledge of the men and things that enter into the problem you have set yourself to solve, then, however you may concentrate, your mental vision will be clouded and indefinite.

Bear in mind that mere recklessness is not an evidence of initiative psychic power. The man who boldly plunges into things does not necessarily possess a high order of concentrative efficiency.

Why not? Simply because a high order of initiative psychic power requires more than a hair-trigger spirit of adventure. It requires vision — vision minute as well as far-seeing.

Do not try to furnish your "castle in Spain" until the foundation is laid, nor lay the foundation until you know the floor plan. Do not set out on your journey until the road is built, nor build the road until you know where it will lead to.

The dreamer is a man of vision, but his vision is of narrow scope. He sees the completed structure, and he revels in its beauty, but he overlooks and sees not at all the ways and means of building it.

The man who does things has a mental vision of them not only as done, but as in the doing. He meets and conquers the obstacles to progress mentally long before the actual emergencies arise.

## STORY OF ONE MAN'S RISE

"That some men rise in a few years from the lowest to the highest positions is always a matter of interest and encouragement to others. One man I recall," says Waldo P. Warren, "is now manager of a large mercantile concern, employing several thousand persons. Eight years ago he began as an office clerk at ten dollars a week. He was unknown to the proprietors, and had neither friend nor relative to aid his advancement."

# GETTING BREADTH OF VIEW

In a case like this it may be necessary to make some allowances for favorable circumstances, but the fact remains that this man was able to fill the higher position. So it must be concluded that it was not circumstances, but some quality of mind, that made him equal to the opportunity. He undoubtedly had integrity, industry and energy. He must also have had judgment, adaptability and tact. But men less successful have had these. He had, however, one very essential quality — comprehensiveness, the ability to grasp the whole plan and purpose of the business and appreciate the relative importance of the various parts. His interest and sympathy were not confined to a mere fragment, but he appreciated the entire business as one great composite idea, and he was constantly expanding that idea. This is the secret of progress, the expansion of thought. This marks the difference between a developer and a mere follower.

## HOW TO APPRAISE A BUSINESS

If you would display initiative psychic power of a high type, study your business not only with reference to its relations with other kinds of business. Make yourself familiar with all its departments, its raw material resources and requirements, its operating units, its cost of production, the quality and quantity of its output, the value and efficiency of its mechanical equipment. Size up your business with reference to others in the same field. Determine the demand, the competition, the best methods of augmenting output and sales, the best systems for arriving at cost of production. Know your business from within and without, so that your sub consciousness is a veritable mine of information concerning it. Then, when you come to put your mind upon creative plans, when you leave the world of facts and go into a self-communion of creative concentration, all these treasures of detail will throng upon you, and, instead of vague dreams, your mind will conjure up a multitude of possibilities, contingencies, emergencies, painting them with life-like clearness of detail. And you will find yourself shrewdly and adroitly assembling your resources to face these contingencies, inventing ways to meet these emergencies, and so unconsciously preparing yourself for the actual problems of your daily life.

## THE LITTLE THINGS IN BUSINESS

You are fully aware of the need of confidence and courage and serene faith. Go, then, a little deeper and you will see that no more satisfying assurance can man have than the knowledge that "everything has been allowed for." It releases untold stores of pent-up reserve energy.

## HOW TO DEVELOP
## FINANCIAL FORESIGHT

If you would develop the foresight that is initiative, you must first of all see things truly as they now are. Only the man of financial foresight can create wealth. And the man of financial foresight possesses an insurance against failure in his knowledge of existing conditions.

Pursue the practice of rigid and thorough investigation in minor matters, and it will serve you faithfully in large affairs.

8. In studying your business, study men.

Men are the tools that the man of psychic power and high initiative works with.

## THE ABILITY TO READ MEN

Study yourself. Analyze the men around you; mark their habits of speech and dress and action in leisure as well as in business hours; mark their behavior under varying conditions.

Choose your enemies with care. Choose your associates with greater care.

## HOW TO CHOOSE A PARTNER

Andrew Carnegie has well said, "He who proves indispensable as a partner to one man might be wholly useless, or even injurious, to another. Generals Grant and Sherman needed very different chiefs of staff. One secret of Napoleon's success arose from his being free to make his own appointments, choosing the men who had the qualities which supplemented his and cured his own shortcomings, for every man has shortcomings. The universal genius who can manage all himself has yet to appear. Only one with the genius to recognize others of different genius and harness them to his own car can approach the universal. It is a case of different but co-operating abilities, each part of the complicated machine fitting into its right place, and there performing its duty without jarring."

To succeed in your undertakings you must tie up with men whose strong points make up for your weak points and whose deficiencies are offset by your strength. Therefore, know the men with whom you propose to associate yourself, their financial resources, their business credit, their personal habits, their past successes, their failures, their elements of strength and weakness. Do they supplement your abilities? Are they your natural complements?

Forearm yourself with facts like these, and then, when you deliberately retire from contact with the world of the senses and give free rein to your creative imagination, and all these men rise up as the human factors in the mental unfolding of your plans, your nimble fancy will correctly gauge their peculiarities, adaptabilities and capabilities, and will assign them suitable parts in your mental drama of creative achievement.

This mental adjustment of the human elements in your problem will find its reflection in your daily life.

## GETTING TEAM-WORK
## INTO A BUSINESS

You will be alert to adapt yourself to the moods of others. You will adjust yourself and your activities to their needs. You will lose sight of petty personalities and differences in your conception of the broader aspects of your undertaking. By thinking it, dreaming it, mentally living it and inwardly realizing it, you will reveal in yourself and beget in others an inner attitude of co-operation. And so will come about that mental harmony, that attitude of all - pull - together - for- the - main - thing that invariably wins its goal.

# THE FIVE EXERCISES FOR CONCENTRATED PSYCHIC POWER AND INITIATIVE

## FOURTH REGIME

### Chapter X

## THE FIVE EXERCISES FOR CONCENTRATED PSYCHIC POWER AND INITIATIVE

## FOURTH REGIME

### CONCERNING PROJECTS, PLANS, INVENTIONS

YOU have analyzed your present mental attitude. You have formulated your desire. You have saturated your mind with relevant facts of observation.

But you must do more, much more, before you will have made the most of your God-given talents and attained to a high degree of mental efficiency.

You must acquire the art of concentration.

You must learn how to focus your forces.

You must possess your mind with purposive thoughts of what you are to have and what you are to be, until new and original conceptions come to you, and come with an impelling force that will not brook postponement.

It is not enough that you should use your energies instead of hoarding them. It is not enough that your life should be a life of action. Your mental energies must be, night and day and unceasingly and purposefully, directed toward a single goal.

# DRAWING POWER FROM WITHOUT

Your mind must reach down into the infinite reservoir and bring forth visions, projects, plans, inventions, devices. It must be filled with the fire of enthusiasm, the cool courage of conviction, and the inventive resourcefulness that is ready for any emergency.

Your mental attitude must be compounded of but two ideas — "I am certain to succeed," and "How?" Consistently and persistently maintaining this attitude, you must draw from the profoundest depths of your being and from all the world about you a constant stream of power, power in the form of initiative thought and power in the form of outside forces working in your interest.

The procedure now to be outlined will enable you to speedily accomplish this result.

# A PROCEDURE FOR DEVELOPING INITIATIVE

Ignorance may whisper, "impossible," "occult," "uncanny." Waste no time on such silly mouthings. You know the underlying scientific principles. You know the power of a concentrated attention. Let the mind, to its innermost subconscious depths, but brood upon a fixed idea, and all the forces of Nature with which you come in touch, within you and without you, will be measured and utilized solely for the realization of that fixed idea, and you will acquire the intensity of desire and the unwavering conviction of its attainment that is creative, dynamic, and carries with it irresistible impulses to efficient activity.

# TWELVE STAR EXERCISES FOR PERSONAL SUPREMACY

First — Every night, half an hour before retiring, go to your room, where you can be entirely alone and as remote as possible from noise and distraction.

Second —Seat yourself in a wide and comfortable chair, or, better still, lie down on your back at full length.

See that your clothing is loosened, so that you will suffer no distressing annoyance on this account. Compose yourself as if for sleep, assuming a position of restfulness, abandon and utter relaxation. Close your eyes, letting the lids rest lightly on your cheeks.

Third — Shut your mind resolutely against every form of bodily sensation. Forget for the time that you are encumbered with a body.

Fourth — Bar out of your consciousness every memory, every thought of the past.

Fifth — Build a mental picture of the thing you want to have, to do or to be – the one thing that you immediately desire first and most of all.

By this we mean nothing indefinite. We do not refer to ultimate aims that can come only as the result of long periods of effort.

We mean something specific, something that can be yours tomorrow, something that in itself constitutes the next step in your chosen career.

Sixth — See yourself finding the ways and means of realizing your desire, overcoming obstacles one after another, all the obstacles that can possibly arise.

See yourself called upon to display, and displaying, alertness, promptness, courage, confidence, resourcefulness, patience, push, enterprise, expert knowledge, insight, shrewdness, tact, self-control, decision.

See yourself face to face with the situation that confronts you in real life and manifesting the qualities and doing the things necessary to your purpose.

Put yourself body and soul into this picture. Multiply details. Rivet your mind upon it.

Seventh — Advance step by step, logically, wisely, consistently, to the climax of the drama.

See yourself winning out. See yourself solving the problem, getting the thing you want, acting the part you desire to play.

Detach your spirit from the flesh of this world and incorporate it in the mental image of yourself.

Live the victory mentally until a sense of its reality permeates your soul.

Eighth — Make your dream picture as delightful as possible. Dwell upon it with joyful satisfaction.

Warm your heart with a feeling of thankfulness that that which you have so long desired is really yours. This feeling of gratitude, this emotional element, will bring forth associations that will give life to the picture and will animate your faith.

Keep yourself tight shut in this dream-world for at least fifteen minutes.

Ninth — Arise and make your preparations for the night. Then upon retiring once more close your eyes and let your mind dwell upon your vision for five or ten minutes or until you fall asleep. Let it be the last thing in your thoughts as you become unconscious.

Tenth — Every time you are awake during the night call the mental picture before you and keep it in consciousness as long as you remain awake.

Eleventh — In the morning, immediately upon awaking, repeat the procedure set out in the third, fourth and fifth instructions.

Twelfth — The more of your spare time you spend in this way, the more promptly will you actualize your ideals. By repeated concentration, every detail of the image of your desire will be so deeply engraved upon your mind as to exert an influence throughout the day. It will inhibit wasteful emotions and impulses. It will give you poise and self-possession. It will so inspire you with its promise as to awaken an energizing response in the profoundest depths of your sub consciousness.

Therefore, practice this exercise of Visualization with reference to the main object of your life night and morning with unwavering regularity. Practice it also at occasional intervals during the day's work whenever any problem of unusual difficulty confronts you. The results of this, simple device will amaze you.

When ideas fail to come, when your work is a tangle of distractions and you know not where to turn, take your troubles into "the silence," and, behold, plans ready-made will come to you, an unsuspected wealth of originality will reveal itself, and you will arise free from doubt, anxiety and fear, and ready to act with decision and confidence!

Visualization is an art. It must be cultivated. It requires incessant practice. And, most important of all, it must have material to work with. It must have facts. It must have an ample fund of detailed information.

## SCOPE OF YOUR PRACTICAL PREVISION

Imagination is based on experience. All your efforts at concentration will be barren of result unless your mental images are clear and life-like counterparts of reality. The play of your creative imagination must deal with men and things truthfully and accurately represented. Only in this way can you prefigure conditions as you will meet, them in the physical world.

You must see in order to foresee.

You must prevision not only ultimate achievements, but ways and means and methods in operation.

You must be possessed with the eternal query, How?

As a publisher, how can you better appeal to the public taste in the make-up of your publications?

As a real estate man, how can you most quickly find a buyer for the land you have to sell?

As a promoter, how can you best explain to the owners of individual enterprises that the promoter's share of stock in the new combination is a legitimate charge, and that your services are needed to bring these diverse interests together?

As an advertiser, how can you frame your advertisement so that ten words will do the work of a thousand and your readers will supply the nine hundred and ninety you have left unsaid?

These eternal "hows" stimulate initiative. Facts coupled with these eternal "hows" are the raw materials you must take with you into the secret chambers of your mind when you retire within yourself and concentrate your mental vision upon the one problem to be solved.

# THE FIVE EXERCISES FOR CONCENTRATED PSYCHIC POWER AND INITIATIVE

## FIFTH REGIME

### Chapter XI

### THE FIVE EXERCISES FOR CONCENTRATED PSYCHIC POWER AND INITIATIVE

### FIFTH REGIME

### SIGHT, FORESIGHT AND OVERSIGHT

TO SUCCEED in a large way, you must be able to see things in clear perspective. You must not only see and foresee, but you must oversee.

---

You cannot do this in a literal sense. The business man who tries to be "all over the place at once" in a physical sense will not get very far. Other men's eyes are yours to use.

## HOW TO ACQUIRE MENTAL UBIQUITY

But mental ubiquity is a faculty that all may acquire.

This exercise will show you how.

First — Follow the first, second, third and fourth instructions given under the preceding exercise. This will bring you to a mood of concentrated attention.

Second — Expand your consciousness by a persistent effort up out of the limits of your body, until you feel yourself to be up above your place of business and able to look down upon all its employees and operations.

Roof, floors, walls hide no secrets from your clairvoyant and clairaudient consciousness. You see at once every inch of the concern. You hear what is being said in every department. You feel yourself in contact with every phase and factor of the enterprise.

## HOW TO RESTORE YOUR
## PSYCHIC BALANCE

Third — Vary this procedure by allowing your consciousness to expand in all directions beyond the limits of your own body and outside the sphere of your personal activities.

In imagination allow your consciousness to widen until it explores the farthest reaches of the heavens. Do not try to form definite thought-pictures. Simply let the mind expand in volume until it seems aware of things far beyond the purview of your body.

Practice this exercise daily for short periods of time. It will develop your imagination. It will lift you out of the petty details of life and restore your psychic balance.

# THE FIVE EXERCISES FOR CONCENTRATED PSYCHIC POWER AND INITIATIVE

## SIXTH REGIME

### Chapter XII

## THE FIVE EXERCISES FOR CONCENTRATED PSYCHIC POWER AND INITIATIVE

## SIXTH REGIME

### SIX EXERCISES IN DELIBERATE AFFIRMATION

WORDS are the expression of thoughts. By incessant repetition words become linked indissolubly with the ideas for which they; stand.

---

So it comes that by our own spoken words we can inspire ourselves even more certainly and effectively than we can inspire others.

This we can do by giving utterance to creative thoughts.

The present exercise indicates the best method for Deliberate Affirmation.

First — Stand erect in the open air or before an open window.

Second — Close your eyes, shut your ears to all sound and disregard everything that may be going on around you.

Third — Breathe very slowly and deeply five times in succession.

Fourth — 'Call forth a feeling of intense energy. Say to yourself, mentally, "I am alert; I am tense and ready; all my faculties are at my instant command; I am charged with courage and expectancy." So far as your body is concerned, there must be no muscle-tension or activity. The sense of energy and expectancy must be restrained and controlled, finding no outward expression.

Fifth — Repeat aloud a few times, quietly but with determined emphasis and with a feeling of intense energy and strength all through your body, the words: "I can and I will succeed in whatever I undertake!"

Sixth — Vary this procedure by affirmation of the following expressions and of others more specific and adapted to your special needs:

"I am equal to this work!"

"I have perfect confidence in myself!"

"I am certain to succeed!"

"I am even now on the way to a great success!"

## TWENTY SELECTED CREATIVE AFFIRMATIONS

"I am successful!"

"I am filled with energy and power!"

"I am brave!"

"My business is growing!"

"My business offers more opportunities today than ever before!"

"Intelligent effort is sure to win in my line of work!"

"My work is just the work I am fitted for!"

"I am happy in my work!"
"I have many friends working for me!"

"Many influences that I know nothing about are at work to help ME win!"

"I am making progress every day!"

"I am well and strong!"

"I am master of my career!"

These sentences embody creative and inspiring thoughts. They will help you to manifest your hidden energies.

They will help you to visualize the object of your desires. They will clear your mental atmosphere and prop your faith.

They will help you more than any conventional prayer, because they are conceived in faith rather than in hope.

# THE FIVE EXERCISES FOR CONCENTRATED PSYCHIC POWER AND INITIATIVE

## SEVENTH REGIME

### Chapter XIII

### THE FIVE EXERCISES FOR CONCENTRATED PSYCHIC POWER AND INITIATIVE

### SEVENTH REGIME

### CULTIVATING THE POWER OF MENTAL DEMAND

THIS is an amplification of the Second Regime, "Formulating a Desire."

You want to succeed. Then, demand success. Demand it with your whole heart and soul and with utmost confidence. And if you have faithfully carried out the regimes set forth in these books, your demand will be speedily and splendidly realized.

## UNCHANGING SEQUENCE OF
## SUCCESS-ACHIEVEMENT

Work as faithfully as you ever did, but affirm more frequently and more fervently, "I am a center of power-creation. I receive power from the universal fund of creative forces. As such a center of power-transmission, I demand that degree of success to which my endowment, my thought and my efforts entitle me. I am sure to succeed in my ambition! My demand is certain to be realized!"

Above all things, remember that in all this work the thought of realization, the mental demand, must precede, not follow, practical outward effort.

Make your affirmations prophetic, not dull statements of fact. Make your psychic energies initiative. Hold fast to this unchanging sequence: first, demand; and by demanding beget Creative Thought; and by creative thinking, Efficient Work; and by efficient working, Win!

# FUNDAMENTALS FOR SELF-ADVANCEMENT

The cultivation of special talents for special pursuits is not within the scope of this Course. For those who desire such special instruction the Society of Applied Psychology is prepared to suggest reading matter suited to each man's individual needs.

But the fundamentals are all here. Therefore, master this book. Study every line.

It may be that at first you will not grasp the full significance of these teachings. But read them again and again. Meditate upon them. Concentrate your thoughts upon them.

## THINGS YOU MUST NOT DO

Soon their eternal truth will dawn upon you, and you will come into the faith that moves mountains.

Read and listen to no conflicting preachments.

Do not attempt to expound these principles to others who have not had your education in the complex processes of the mind and would fail to understand.

Do not concern yourself with occult or spiritual forces. You know the secret of these so-called mysteries. All forces are within you.

The whole science of success is in this book. Follow the instructions of this lesson, and you cannot fail to get the thing you want. You are sure of success.

# THE ELIXIR OF MENTAL LIFE

Therefore, do not wait for things to be a little different. Do not postpone action until a more opportune time. One day is like another. Act now. Wealth and power are within your grasp.

Endless avenues of self-advancement open before you. There are evil desires to be strangled in their birth. There are wasteful and soul-destroying habits to be eradicated. There are pleasures that beckon — foolish, vain and trivial pleasures. There are voices to be stilled — voices of regret and secret shame that call to you out of the past.

Practice self-concentration and self-inspiration, and you may go forth each day unhampered by impulses that would compromise your standing or by thoughts that would pollute your soul.

Have you been blighted by the chill winds of disaster? Have you fallen from the ladder of life to lie stunned and inert in the slime of despair? Have you lost the hope that gives life to ambition and zest to pursuit? Do you lack the courage to endure and do? To you we give a precious elixir. It is a strengthening, exhilarating, exalting instrumentality of wondrous power. It will make you a healthier, a wiser, a happier, a more successful man.